Our Journey from Tibet

BASED ON A TRUE STORY

by Laurie Dolphin

photographs by
Nancy Jo Johnson

WITH A LETTER FROM HIS HOLINESS
THE DALAI LAMA
AND AN AFTERWORD BY RINCHEN K. CHOEGYAL

Dutton Children's Books ✦ New York

For information about how you can help improve the health and education of Tibetan children living in India, Nepal, and Tibet, please contact:

The Tibet Fund
241 East 32nd Street
New York, New York 10016
phone: 212–213–5011
fax: 212–779–9245
E-mail: otny@igc.apc.org

The Tibet Fund is a nonprofit, charitable organization dedicated to preserving Tibetan culture and improving all aspects of life for Tibetan refugees and Tibetans living inside Tibet. One of the many projects the Tibet Fund supports is education for Tibetan children. The Department of Education and the Tibetan Children's Village educate and care for more than 30,000 orphans and destitute children, providing them with shelter, security, and plenty of love. Please contact the Tibet Fund for information on how you can sponsor a child and about other projects that help the neediest.

A PORTION OF THE AUTHOR'S ROYALTIES FROM THIS BOOK WILL BE USED TO BENEFIT TIBETAN CHILDREN IN EXILE.

CIP Data is available.

Published in the United States by Dutton Children's Books,
a division of Penguin Books USA Inc.
375 Hudson Street, New York, New York 10014

Designed by Semadar Megged
Printed in U.S.A.   First Edition
ISBN 0-525-45577-9
1 3 5 7 9 10 8 6 4 2

To my parents, with appreciation for their kindness and good hearts!

L.D.

To the children in my life: Dhundup Tsering; Blake Herendeen; Jackson and Jordan Ferrick; Lily and Oliver DiCostanzo; Abigail, Maggie, and Jessica Pucker; and to my parents, Don and Gerry Johnson

N.J.J.

The photographer and the author standing with His Holiness the Fourteenth Dalai Lama

✚ A C K N O W L E D G M E N T S ✚

We would like to express our gratitude to those who helped in the telling of this story:

His Holiness the Dalai Lama • Sonam, Dekyi, and Payang (the sisters of Sog Dzong) •
Tenzin P. Atisha, Director, Environment and Development, Department of Information and International Relations •
Rinchen K. Choegyal, Minister-in-Charge for Education, for her support and information •
Rinchen Dharlo, Representative of His Holiness the Dalai Lama for the Americas (Without his assistance, this book would not have been possible.) • Diane DiCostanzo • Tashi Dolma, for her guidance, patience, and time • Dianne Dubler •
Anthony Kastellic • Debra Ladner and Pema Wangdak • Karen Lotz • Michel Madie • Michele McNally •
Semadar Megged • William Nabers • Michelle Poiré • Gigi Pucker • Nina Reznick • Comfort Shields •
John Bigelow Taylor • Tenzin Geyshe Tethong, Secretary to His Holiness the Dalai Lama • Gompo Tsering •
Tempa Tsering, General Secretary, Department of Information and International Relations • Lama Pema Wangdak •
Kalsang Wangdue, Pema B. Tesur, Reverend Pema Dorjee, Karma Dolker •
And finally we wish to thank Ufuk Omer Arkun and Miles and Brian Dolphin for their junior editing skills.

My name is Sonam.

Whenever I see the snowcapped mountains, I remember my family. It's been more than two years, but in my mind I can clearly see my grandmother, my mom and dad, my uncle, my brothers, and our beautiful homeland, Tibet, the Land of Snows.

Somehow, looking at these mountains comforts me. I know that right behind them lies the land where I was born.

Let me tell you our story of how and why we left our home.

More than forty years ago, our neighbors, the Chinese, took over our country. This was done with force and cruelty.

I wasn't yet born when this happened, but the scars on our land tell the story. All over Tibet, monasteries were destroyed—more than six thousand of them. Monasteries are places where we pray. Inside are sacred religious objects and writings. All of this was destroyed. Now what remains looks like piles of rock.

Religion is a very important part of Tibetan life, so for us this was tragic.

When I was younger, I didn't see many Chinese. I lived in a small Tibetan village, Sog Dzong, which is northeast of Lhasa, our capital city. Our home was a traditional Tibetan house made of mud bricks. We owned lots of animals. We had thirty yaks, forty sheep, and two horses. From the yaks, we got our butter and milk. From their hair, we made our clothing, and from their dung, we kept our homes warm. These are traditional Tibetan ways.

By law, the Chinese are allowed to have only one child per family. Tibetans normally have large families. I have four brothers and two sisters. None of us went regularly to school in Tibet. For us, it was too expensive.

For one month, though, my parents were able to afford it. I remember that pictures of Communist leaders hung on the walls of our classroom. When I told my mom and dad about these pictures, they reminded me that these were not my leaders.

His Holiness the Dalai Lama is both our spiritual and our political leader. He wants Tibet to be free from Chinese rule, but he does not want us to use force or weapons to accomplish this. He believes in kindness, compassion, and *sem zangpo* (having a good heart). All Tibetans are devoted to him.

During the Chinese takeover, His Holiness fled from Tibet because his life was in danger. Now he lives in India and leads the Tibetan government-in-exile. When our homeland is free and our people are happy, he will return home.

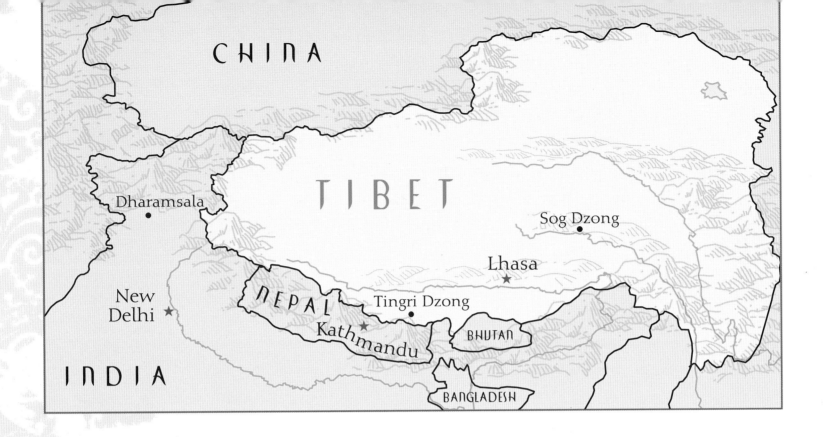

Under the Chinese occupation, Tibetans are not happy in their homeland. There is no freedom of speech. Many Tibetans, even monks and nuns, have been put in prison and tortured for speaking the truth. The Chinese control both our worship and our education. Because of this, my parents became very concerned about our family's future.

Ngawang, my second-eldest brother, was the first in our family to escape Tibet. He left for India to become a monk. It is a Tibetan tradition that the middle son becomes a monk.

After one year, Ngawang returned to our home with important news. This news changed my life.

He told us that in Dharamsala, India, he had visited wonderful Tibetan schools that taught exiled Tibetan children about their culture and their history. These schools were free.

"Even His Holiness the Dalai Lama lives in Dharamsala," my brother told us. "For the good future of my sisters, I believe they should go to these schools."

That day, it was decided that Dekyi, Payang, and I would escape and take the illegal journey out of Tibet into India. My parents would stay behind to take care of my grandmother. We would travel with Ngawang and a paid driver.

Inside, I was shaken up. My stomach was in knots. I knew that I might not see my parents or return to my home ever again.

Outside our village is a sacred lake. For comfort, I went to it. As I looked into its blue waters, a deep peace filled my body. I prayed that soon I would see His Holiness the Dalai Lama. This thought made me feel happy and calm.

When I walked home, I saw my grandma and my friends gathered together. They wanted to play. Everything seemed the same, but inside, I felt different. I was ready to take this journey.

At dusk, we left by truck. Dekyi, Payang, and I rode in the back of the truck, sitting on sacks of salt. Ngawang sat up front with the driver.

We took very little with us: an extra set of clothes, blankets, and some bread, cheese, butter, and *tsampa* (a flour made from ground roasted barley).

Our driver was paid six thousand yuans (seven hundred dollars) to take us to the mountain pass.

All through the night, we drove. The next day, we passed through a big thunderstorm. At the end of the storm, we saw a beautiful rainbow.

"This is auspicious!" Ngawang said. "Perhaps this means a high lama is being born, or maybe one has passed away." Tibetans believe that phenomena such as rainbows and thunder are caused by deities who want to mark an event. For example, if it rains after a celebration, Tibetans believe this is an omen that the mountain deities are happy.

I hoped this beautiful rainbow meant that our journey would be a safe one.

During the drive, we were always afraid of being caught by the Chinese. We knew that we were leaving Tibet without Chinese permission and without permits. At checkpoints, the Chinese ask to see these permits.

If we were caught without them, we feared that we might be beaten or sent to prison, and we also might get the rest of our family in trouble.

Each time before we got to a checkpoint, our driver would stop and hide all three of us inside the sacks of salt piled in the back of the truck. Whenever we felt the truck stop for a search, my heart would be in my throat. Every minute seemed like an hour. We could hear the Chinese soldiers talking. They would go to the back of the truck and look in, but luckily, each time they left us alone.

When our truck would finally drive away, all of us would giggle with relief and joy.

Our driver was paid only to drive us to the mountain pass. In the valley just before the mountains, he let us out. There we found a guide with other children. Ngawang gave this guide more money for the next part of our journey.

Before we started, we washed ourselves in the river. Then we gathered together, boiled the river water, and prepared a tea ceremony as an offering.

All of us prayed to the local mountain deities for their protection.

Together we walked toward the snowcapped Himalaya Mountains. We walked from early in the morning before sunrise until late at night. We walked until our feet were numb and swollen and our shoes were torn.

Sometimes we had to cross streams and rivers. This was frightening. It was easy to slip.

Eventually we ran out of food. Luckily, before we reached the snows, we met some *drokpas* (nomads), and they sold us some food. At this mountain pass, there were lots of prayer flags. These are cloths printed with prayers. The wind carries the prayers over the land.

Once again, we stopped to pray.

Ngawang warned us that the next part of the journey would be awful. We would be walking through the snow.

He was right. At night, we slept in caves. I imagined that wild animals might come and gobble us up. In these caves, we would make fires to warm our feet and cook our food. We melted ice to make our tea. It tasted strange.

One boy in our group could no longer walk. His foot had turned black, and our guide told us this was called frostbite. We all took turns helping him.

The sun that warmed us also harmed us. Our eyes burned from its glare. To protect us from snow blindness, Payang cut her hair and gave us strands to wrap around our foreheads. These shades did help, but nothing could protect us from the sting of the wind and the cold of the air.

At one very high peak, I looked back at my homeland and said a silent good-bye.

Our descent was easier. The air began to get warmer. The snow disappeared, and the earth became muddy and slippery. Our feet slid easily down the mountainside.

We were told that soon we would reach the last checkpoint, Friendship Bridge. This bridge connects Tibet to Nepal.

At this checkpoint, our guide spoke to the Chinese and paid them money. Then we were allowed to sneak over. The Chinese soldier didn't even look our way. When we entered Nepal, our guide spoke to the Nepalese guards and gave them some more money.

From then on, our hearts were happy. We were in a new and beautiful land. Waterfalls cascaded down the mountains. It was green everywhere. The land was covered with evergreen trees and moss. For us, this was a drastic change. We were used to the bare mountains of Tibet.

When our guide escorted us to a Nepalese bus, we were relieved to know that our walking journey was over. We were told that we would be traveling by bus through Nepal to the Tibetan Reception Center.

All through the bus ride, my eyes were glued to the window. Everything was different. The land was fertile. We passed miles of water-filled rice paddies. The homes were made of red brick. I saw my first cow, and all the people looked very different.

Ngawang said that at the Reception Center, we would be interviewed, fingerprinted, and given papers to go to Dharamsala, India.

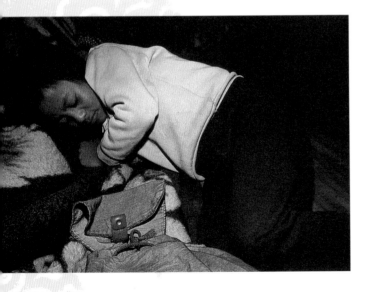

Smiling Tibetan faces greeted us when we got to Kathmandu, and the workers and volunteers immediately took care of my group. They put salve on our badly infected, peeling skin. The boy with frostbite was given medical care. A delicious meal was served, and I slept well for the first time in over a month.

For a few days, we waited with little to do. Finally, a bus came to take us to New Delhi, India. In the early morning we traveled, and I saw for the first time what the sun looks like when it rises above a flat horizon. It was magical.

For three days, we rode on this bus. In New Delhi, our papers were stamped again, and a new bus came to take us to Dharamsala. Ngawang told us that now we were close to the end of our journey.

I was so excited. All I could think about was seeing His Holiness the Dalai Lama. This thought alone made the one-day ride whiz by.

Dharamsala lies at the top of a mountain. As our bus circled endlessly up the hill, I was reminded of our own Tibetan mountains.

When the bus stopped, we all stepped out into a downpour and were received by a kind Tibetan man who gave us umbrellas and walked us to the Tibetan Reception Center.

At this center, it was confirmed that Dekyi, Payang, and I would be going to school together at the Tibetan Children's Village. We were delighted.

However, soon Ngawang had to return to the monastery of Sera in southern India.

When it was time for him to leave us, we were all unbearably sad. But we tried to be cheerful, which is the Tibetan way. We told him that we would write. We smiled, but after he was gone, our true feelings rose to the surface. Dekyi's face remained sad for days.

We were told that soon we would be going to our new home and school, but before that we would have the opportunity to meet His Holiness the Dalai Lama. Like the changing weather, our spirits brightened. When we went for a walk, we passed prayer wheels and turned them clockwise. I said prayers of thanks!

My dream was about to come true. I knew that so many Tibetans at home longed to meet His Holiness. The fact that this good fortune had come to me seemed miraculous.

On the day of our meeting, we were given white *khatas* (offering scarves). All the people staying at the Tibetan Reception Center were taken to the place where His Holiness resides. Then we all stood on line and waited for a long time. As we approached him, I became so nervous that I could hardly breathe.

Finally it was my turn to meet him. When he saw me, his hands touched my head. I relaxed immediately. His smile and warmhearted laugh made me smile and feel so happy. This happiness lasted the whole day.

After that, something changed inside me. I understood that my life would have its ups and downs, happiness and hardship, but I had a future.

My future would live in my spirit, and my spirit, like His Holiness, would radiate kindness and a good heart. This is our Tibetan way.

When my sisters and I at last entered the gates of the Tibetan Children's Village, we were welcomed warmly. "Others Before Self" is the motto of this village, and you can feel it when you live here.

In my home, I live with my sisters and many other Tibetan children. We do everything together. We prepare our meals, take baths, clean our home, play, and study together. My family would be so proud to see how I've grown up.

Kindness is contagious. In the village, the older kids always help the younger ones. Even my sisters and I don't fight anymore.

Payang, Dekyi, and I have lived in the Tibetan Children's Village for over two years. All the children here have taken a similar journey from Tibet to India. We all have this in common, but I am learning that we share much more—our language, our religion, our history, and our united longing to return to our homeland, to a free Tibet.

Dekyi

Sonam

Payang

Many children from Tibet, in order to receive quality education and a spiritually stable environment, have taken refuge in Tibetan schools in exile.

The journey from Tibet to Nepal and India, as shown in this book, is often treacherous and risky. I am particularly moved to meet children who have escaped from Tibet and to hear about all the risks they have taken to receive an education uncontaminated by Chinese Communist propaganda. Under the Chinese occupation of Tibet, freedom to travel is not permissible, and children are endangering themselves and their families by escaping. Parents and children take these risks, however, because they feel that schools in Tibet do not impart the sort of education that will guarantee the survival of the Tibetan nation and the preservation of its culture and identity.

Under the Chinese colonization, Tibetans have been reduced to second-class citizens in their own homeland. Chinese has become the official language of instruction in the schools, and Tibetan history and its culture are generally disregarded in education. The teachers that teach Tibetans often do not have qualified backgrounds. In the nomadic areas of Tibet, children virtually do not have schools.

In order to rectify this bleak situation, children flee from Tibet in search of a hopeful future, where they will be able to learn more about their own cultural heritage and identity, besides receiving quality education in general modern studies.

It is my hope that these children, once educated, will soon be able to return to their homeland and share their cultural understanding and education with their families and compatriots. From the very first day we became refugees, be it concerning the future of our nation or an individual Tibetan family or the community, one of the most important priorities has been to impart and improve the education of the Tibetans by establishing special schools with both modern and Tibetan characteristics.

I am confident that this book, backed by pictures, will benefit the children of the world in giving them a better understanding of what is happening to Tibetan children and their culture.

TENZIN GYATSO
His Holiness the Fourteenth Dalai Lama

A F T E R W O R D

A vast majority of children in Tibet continue to be deprived of the opportunity for even very basic education as enshrined in the United Nations Charter on the Rights of the Child. After more than four decades of occupation, the Chinese authorities continue relentlessly in their efforts to systematically destroy all facets of Tibetan identity, targeting the youth in particular. To counter this, the Tibetans in exile under the guidance of His Holiness the Dalai Lama have over the last thirty-five years established scores of schools and institutions providing quality modern education to the younger generation while at the same time promoting the learning of Tibetan language, literature, history, music, and the performing arts. To keep alive our Buddhist religious traditions, many monastic institutions that were destroyed in Tibet under the Chinese have been reestablished in exile and are thriving.

RINCHEN K. CHOEGYAL
Minister-in-Charge for Education

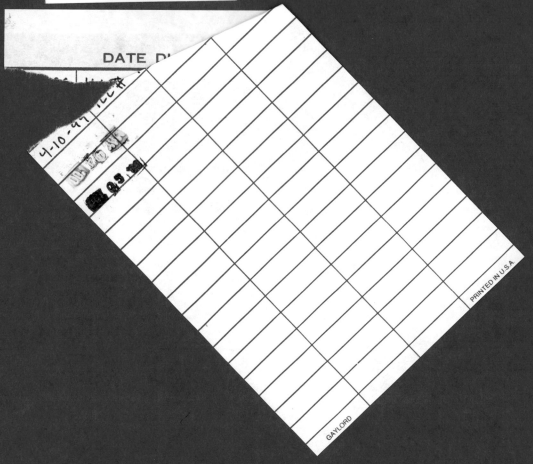